Happy Hearts

Ron and Rebekah Coriell

Published Under Arrangement with
Fleming H. Revell Co. by

A publication of
ASSOCIATION OF CHRISTIAN SCHOOLS INTERNATIONAL

P.O. BOX 4097, WHITTIER, CA 90607

Diligent

sent

Working Hard to Accomplish a Task

Seest thou a man diligent in his business? He shall stand before kings. . . .

Proverbs 22:29

Diligence in the Bible

Who could these men be, walking the streets of Jerusalem so late at night? They seemed to know each other, because they stayed together and talked quietly among themselves. One man seemed to be their leader. They made their way, past dark houses and the closed shops, toward the city gate. They walked away from Jerusalem, toward a garden called Gethsemane. As they entered the garden, Jesus asked eight men to stay behind and took three men with Him, farther in among the trees. He had often prayed in this garden, and He knew just where He wanted to speak with His heavenly Father. This night's prayer would be one of the hardest of His life.

Peter, James, and John sat down. Jesus walked farther and fell to His knees. So earnest was His prayer that blood dripped from His forehead. An hour later, He returned to His three friends, to see if they had prayed with Him. No, they had fallen asleep.

Jesus could have joined them in rest, but He had much to say to His Father. Again He prayed. He knew that soon He would be betrayed by Judas, tried, convicted, and finally crucified. Yet, Jesus worked hard to finish His second prayer. His disciples continued to sleep as Jesus diligently prayed a third time.

Our Saviour could have done many other things to prepare Himself for the dreadful events that followed; but, instead, He chose hours of diligent prayer to strengthen Himself.

Diligence at Home

"Can I go, too?" pleaded Danny Ellis.

His brother, Darin, responded, "No, you'd better stay home. Chopping and carrying firewood are hard work. You are too young and too little."

Danny frowned. With a hurt look in his eyes, he pulled on his father's pant leg.

"Father, I can work almost as hard as Darin. Please give me a chance," said Danny.

"All right, Son," replied Mr. Ellis. "It is hot, and the wood is heavy, so you must take it easy today."

All three climbed into the truck and drove to a farm. Mr. Ellis had been given five trees to cut down and remove. Chopping down the trees was Mr. Ellis's job. Darin cut the limbs off, and Danny was assigned to stack the wood into big piles. After two hours of work, his father and brother took a rest break, but Danny still felt strong.

"You two just take it easy. I will keep working a little longer," he insisted.

Darin and his father looked at each other in surprise. They did not think Danny would be so diligent at the hard work. The job was completed, and all the wood was stacked in the truck.

"Let's all go get a milk shake," said Mr. Ellis, winking at Darin. "I think Danny the Diligent deserves it."

Diligence at School

"I am afraid Danny is a little behind his classmates in reading," said the teacher.

"We expected this when we moved Danny to this Christian school," explained his father. "It is our hope that he will work hard to catch up to the rest of the children. Do you think you can do it, Dan?"

"I will try my best, Daddy," he replied with excitement.

Danny Ellis's new school was special. Children came from all over the city to be enrolled. Teachers and students worked together to do their best. Danny was glad to be able to attend such a school. Yet he also realized that much hard work was ahead.

Two weeks later, Danny's school had an open house. Many parents came to meet the teachers and see some of their children's work. Danny's father was especially interested in talking with Danny's teacher. "How is my boy doing in his schoolwork?" Mr. Ellis asked.

With a smile of approval at Danny, the teacher responded, "Danny has had to work very hard. I am glad to say he has become a very good reader. It is his diligence that has helped him to improve so much."

"Danny has become diligent since he became a Christian," responded Mr. Ellis. "Now he wants to

Diligence at Play

Crack! The baseball flew across the backyard. Danny's older brother, Darin, had hit another home run. With a big smile, he ran around the bases.

Now, it was Danny's turn. He gripped the bat tightly. Father pitched a ball over home plate. Danny swung with all his might, but missed the ball. Darin began to giggle.

Father cautioned, "Darin, it is not kind to giggle. You should be encouraging your younger brother. Danny, let's try it again."

With a deep sigh, Danny picked up his bat and waited for Father to pitch the ball. Tears filled his eyes.

Angrily, Danny dropped his bat and cried, "I quit!" Away he ran, to the back steps.

Father excused himself from the game and joined his son. "Son, you are not giving up, are you?" asked Father.

"I tried, but I can't hit the ball," Danny explained.

Then, Father reminded him, "Diligence means you don't give up. You must keep trying, even if you don't feel like it. The Lord is interested in your problem, Danny. Let's pray about it."

Danny asked the Lord to help him to keep trying and to have the courage he needed when it was his turn to bat.

How happy the family was to have Danny rejoin the game and diligently play baseball.

Patient

rent

Waiting With A Happy Spirit

Be ye also patient; stablish your hearts. . . .

James 5:8

Patience in the Bible

Jesus' disciples were shocked at His words. They had followed the Saviour for nearly three years. They had forsaken all to serve Him. Now, He was telling them that they would soon leave Him.

Jesus said, "All ye shall be offended because of Me this night."

Peter spoke up, firmly, in protest. "Though all men shall be offended because of You, I will never be offended. Lord, I am ready to go with You, both into prison and to death."

A few hours later, Jesus was arrested, by a mob of angry men, in the Garden of Gethsemane. Just as Jesus had said, all His disciples ran away. No one stayed to help Him, not even Peter. As Jesus was taken to the high priest's house, Peter followed and joined some people warming themselves by a fire. At three different times, people told him that he looked like one of Jesus' disciples. Peter lied and denied even knowing Jesus.

As the rooster crowed a welcome to the new day, the Lord Jesus turned and looked upon Peter. Then Peter remembered the words of Jesus: "Before the cock crows you will deny Me three times."

Jesus loved Peter very much. Even though he had denied Him three times, He was willing to wait for Peter to become a faithful servant. Peter later became one of the greatest preachers of all time. The patience of Jesus was rewarded.

Patience at Home

"Mother's spaghetti!" shrieked Patty. "It's my favorite!"

Her mother smiled. "I knew you would be happy. Your father has worked very hard today, fixing the car. He is going to enjoy it, too."

Quickly, Patty ran to the backyard. She called her two younger sisters and hurriedly helped them to wash for dinner. Then they helped set the table and sat down.

"Why are we waiting?" questioned Patty.

"Well," responded Mother, "I called your father just a minute ago. He said he was coming. Let's be polite and wait patiently until everyone gets to the table."

Patty folded her hands in her lap, and so did her sisters. Mother kept working in the kitchen to prepare the last few details of the meal.

Watching the steam rise from the spaghetti, Patty thought, *I wish Father would hurry. Spaghetti is only good when it is hot.*

Moments passed that seemed like hours. Her sisters began to wiggle.

Anxiously, they asked, "May we eat now, Mother?"

"No, not until Father gets here," she said. "He will be finished soon. Please wait with happy spirits."

Just then, Father walked in with a big smile on his greasy face. "Thank you, girls," he said, "for being so patient."

Patience at School

Patty burst into the classroom. "He's bleeding, he's bleeding!" she shouted.

Startled, Mrs. Kelly jumped up from her desk and hurried into the hall. A crowd of children was standing around the drinking fountain.

"Please stand back, children. Let me have some room," she said firmly.

As the children parted, she saw Robbie, in the center, holding his mouth. Blood was trickling down between his fingers and onto the floor.

"What happened?" asked Mrs. Kelly.

"Well," said Patty, all out of breath, "We were all waiting in line for a drink. Someone at the end of the line pushed, and we all bumped into one another. Robbie was drinking and hit his tooth on the drinking fountain."

Gently wiping away the blood, Mrs. Kelly opened Robbie's mouth to see how badly his lip was cut. She carefully applied a cold towel to his lip, to prevent any swelling.

"You will be fine, Robbie," she said calmly. "There is only a small cut in your lip. Your tooth looks all right."

The children all looked at the floor when she turned to them. "We are very fortunate," she said, "that Robbie was not injured more seriously. Not being patient can cause someone to get injured. Let's remember this lesson, so that no one ever gets hurt at the drinking fountain again."

Patience at Play

I wonder if the paint is dry enough, thought Patty. *Mother said to wait until after supper.*

Circling the freshly painted swing set, she was careful not to let her dress touch the metal. How it glistened in the sun, with its shiny new coat of red paint!

Maybe, if I just touch it with one finger, she said to herself, *then I would know if it is still wet.*

Cautiously, she reached out her finger. Then, quickly, she pulled it back.

Mother said this paint only comes off with smelly paint remover. I would hate to have to wash my hands with that, thought Patty.

Again she walked around the swing, studying it closely. *I could touch it with a piece of paper*, she reasoned. *If no red paint came off, I would know that it was dry.*

Patty quickly found a stick and wrapped some old newspaper on it. Before she tried it, she changed her mind.

If the swing is still wet, the paper will stick to it and leave a mark, Patty remembered.

So, with a sigh, she decided to wait patiently until after supper. As she was helping with the dishes, her mother said, "Patty, I know it has been hard to wait with a happy spirit for the paint to dry. Because you have been so patient, you may have some ice cream when you have finished swinging."

Content
dent

Happy With What I Have

But godliness with contentment is great gain.

1 Timothy 6:6

Contentment in the Bible

"Master, I will follow You wherever You go." These were strange words for a scribe to say to Jesus.

A scribe was one of the few people in Bible times who knew how to read and write. He studied the Scripture and taught it to others. Some were lawyers and judges; therefore, scribes were usually wealthy, respected, and lived in nice homes.

Jesus knew that this scribe did not really mean what he said. He would not be content to live like Jesus. So the Lord replied, "The foxes have holes, and the birds have nests, but the Son of man doesn't have anywhere to lay His head."

By this, Jesus meant that even birds and animals have homes. But the Saviour didn't have a house to go home to after preaching and healing during the day. Before He came to earth, His home was in heaven. On earth, He was content to sleep outside, under the trees or in caves.

The Bible does not tell us if the scribe followed Jesus. Perhaps he was not willing to give up the nice house he lived in and sleep outside with the Master.

Jesus knew how the scribe really felt in his heart. Today, Jesus knows how happy we are with what we have. It is important that we be content, because the Bible says, "Godliness with contentment is great gain" (1 Timothy 6:6).

Contentment at Home

Connie came out of her room, with a disturbed look on her face. "Mother, I must have new shoes for school," she said.

Looking up from her dusting, Mother told Connie that her feet had not grown enough, this summer, to make new leather shoes necessary. She would have to wear last year's school shoes, because they still fit.

Connie walked back to her room, mumbling, "All the other girls will look pretty with new shoes, and I will just have these ugly old things to wear. I won't be pretty."

The night before school began, Father polished Connie's shoes. "There, they look much better," he said.

Connie still frowned. Mother reminded her that if she really wanted to look pretty for school, she would need the right spirit. "Real beauty comes from having a happy heart," she said.

The next morning, they prayed that Connie would be content with her old shoes and that she would be happy. God answered their prayer, because Connie really enjoyed her first day of school.

Mother was pleased to see her big smile as she arrived home. "I guess you were right, Mother," said Connie. "Having the right spirit makes you content. No one noticed that I didn't have new shoes."

Contentment at School

Connie frowned as she was passed a box of crayons. *These are old, broken ones,* she thought.

As she emptied the crayon box on her desk, Connie saw unbroken green and brown crayons, one-half of a blue and a yellow, and only tiny parts of red and orange crayons. None of the crayons had wrappers around them. She looked with envy at some of the other children, who had new crayons. It seemed unfair for her to get the old crayons to use. Yet she knew there were not enough new boxes of crayons to go around. This time it was her turn to use the old ones.

A Bible verse she had learned at vacation Bible school helped her to be content. She remembered that it said, "Godliness with contentment is great gain." So, without complaint, she began her drawing.

She used the green and the brown crayons to make trees and the ground. Because they did not have paper around them, she was able to use the side of the crayons to fill in the picture. The half-sized blue crayon was just large enough to color between her tree leaves, and the small yellow one was perfect for coloring small flowers. The red crayon had a jagged edge which made it easy to draw thin, red bird wings. And she used the orange to color in a bright sun.

"What a creative picture," said Miss Cooper, the teacher.

Smiling inside, Connie thought, *It really does help to be content and creative with what you have.*

Contentment at Play

Connie jumped out of bed as the alarm clock rang. *I hope it is not raining today. Mother is taking me to the beach, to learn how to swim,* she thought.

As Connie pulled back her curtains, her joy turned to gloom. All she could see were hundreds of sparkling beads of water, running down the glass pane.

"Now, I will never be able to swim," she moaned.

Sadly, she dressed and went downstairs for breakfast. Noticing her sad spirit, her mother asked, "Why are you so gloomy today?"

"You should see the weather," Connie replied. "It is wet, dark, and cold. I just know the beach will be closed."

"I know you are unhappy," said Mother, "but you can't let this make you sad all day. You must be content to not swim today. Maybe tomorrow will be sunny."

As the family ate breakfast, Connie's father talked about how Jesus was happy with what He had. He left the beauty of heaven and was content to be born in a stable. He could have been a king, but He was happy as a servant to others. He could have lived in a mansion; however, He was content to never own a house.

Connie wanted to be like Jesus. With a smile, she said, "I will be content and happy, even if I can't learn to swim today."

Primary Character Challenges

Here are some practical suggestions that will reinforce the concepts taught in the preceding stories.

Diligence

1. Proverbs 6:6–8 teaches that the ant is diligent. Observe and consider an ant's life.
2. Read the story of Jacob, in Genesis 29. How did he work hard to marry his wife?
3. Romans 12:12 says, ". . . continuing instant [diligently] in prayer." Find a prayer request, pray diligently, and continue until God answers your prayer.

Patience

1. Play a game with the child. Encourage patience as he waits for his turn.
2. Find out to whom we are to show patience. Look up Psalms 37:7 and 1 Thessalonians 5:14.
3. Help the child memorize 1 Thessalonians 5:14.

Contentment

1. Teach the child to find blessings in an area in which he is not content.
2. Help the child memorize 1 Timothy 6:6.
3. List the things that God promises will last for eternity, in the following verses: Isaiah 40:8, Matthew 6:19-21, Psalms 90:2, and Hebrews 13:8.